YOUR KNOWLEDGE HAS VALUE

Mehmet Sarialtin

The Significance of Innovation for Business

GRIN Verlag

Bibliografische Information der Deutschen Nationalbibliothek:

Die Deutsche Bibliothek verzeichnet diese Publikation in der Deutschen National-
bibliografie; detaillierte bibliografische Daten sind im Internet über http://dnb.d-
nb.de/ abrufbar.

Imprint:

Copyright © 2011 GRIN Verlag GmbH
Druck und Bindung: Books on Demand GmbH, Norderstedt Germany
ISBN: 978-3-656-35528-1

This book at GRIN:

http://www.grin.com/en/e-book/206823/the-significance-of-innovation-for-business

Table of Contents

1. Introduction
    1.1. Purpose
    1.2. Limitations and method
    1.3. Scope

2. Declaration of innovation
    2.1. Definition of innovation
    2.2. Types of innovation
        2.2.1. Product innovation
        2.2.2. Process innovation
        2.2.3. Market innovation

3. A successful innovator
    3.1. Apple Inc. as an exemplary model
    3.2. The correlation between Apple's innovative
          product range and success

4. Innovation and change
    4.1. The differences between innovation and change
    4.2. The similarities between innovation and change

5. Conclusion

6. List of reference

1. Introduction

1.1 Purpose

Innovation represents a strong growth engine for almost all companies in different branches. In particular global, but also domestically operating companies, have to perceive the development of new services, products and processes as a prerequisite for a successful going concern, because it is the main reason why companies can still compete in the future market. The purpose of this essay is to explain the significance of innovation for business, because more and more companies cannot withstand the pressure through innovation within branches.

1.2. Limitations and method

The type of analysis used was the selection and evaluation of three chosen journal articles from Emerald, the textbook and other academic sources for theory based content.

1.3. Scope

The Scope of the essay will look at the significance of innovation by giving a definition of innovation and an example from the company Apple Inc., subsequently outlines the differences between innovation and change and finally concludes with the key decisions.

2. Declaration of innovation

2.1. Definition of innovation

Since the history of mankind innovations play a significant role and sometimes also social conditions encouraged the emergence of innovations, especially in crises. Innovations can be searched systematically or may occur randomly. Systematically created innovations are combined with a deliberate research and development. Innovations by random are certainly equally important, one of the most popular example are the penicillin, which is one of the oldest antibiotic and helped to save countless live.

Nevertheless, "Industrial innovation includes the technical, design, manufacturing, management and commercial activities involved in the marketing of a new (or improved) product or the first commercial use of a new (or improved)process or equipment" (Chris Freeman, 1982, The Economics of Industrial Innovation, 2nd edition, Printer, London).

Thus innovations can be defined as the first commercial exploitation of an invention by producing and marketing a new product or a new process in production.

At this point Figure 1 helps to understand the context between invention and innovation,

The capacity for innovation is also important to create a value. Modes of thinking and behaviour patterns are more open. Innovations stimulate the imagination of the shareholders, because they promise positive prospective earnings.

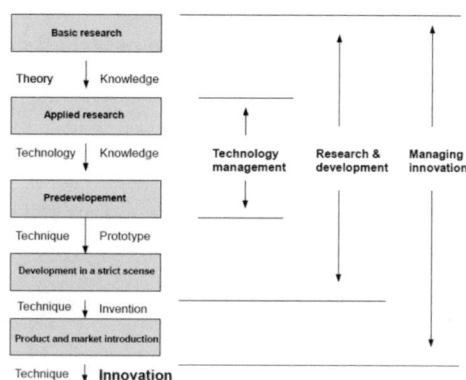

Figure 1, Invention and innovation

Social innovations can be defined as non- technological innovations and are concerned with human behaviour, for example, new approaches to working time regulations, or new approaches to increase job satisfaction.

2.2. Types of innovation

2.2.1. Product innovation

Human needs are technically unlimited and change constantly. Product innovations try to counteract and satisfy needs and are necessary, because demand preferences change. It is the development of a new product through the consideration of new technological trends. The iPhone from Apple Inc. can be considered as an example for a successful product innovation.

2.2.2. Process innovation

Innovations of a company, which are related to the process of service provision, can be described as a process innovation. For instance, this could be a latest accounting software, a new method of metal working or if banking transactions are being done by mobile phone.

The target of a process innovation is the increase of productivity through the development of a production or service process and the improvement of cost saving within a company. Consequently, a process innovation can increase the efficiency and effectiveness of service provision.

2.2.3 Market innovation

Market innovation aims to identify better and newer potential markets and possibilities to serve novel target markets.

Furthermore, it deals with the best choice and service of markets, but also with the improvement of the mix of target markets. The identification of the target markets is possible through an ideally market segmentation. This implies that "Market segmentation, which involves dividing a total potential market into smaller more manageable parts, is critically important if the aim is to develop the profitability of a business to the full. Incomplete market segmentation will result in a less than optimal mix of target markets, meaning that revenues which might have been earned are misread" (Axel John, 1999, Successful market innovation, European Journal of Innovation Management, Volume 2 , Number 1, p6-11)

3. A successful innovator

3.1. Apple Inc. as an exemplary model

It seems like Apple Inc. has magic power and everything, which is being touched by the management, turns into gold. Apple Inc. has no magic wand. The company is just refocused on the wishes of customers. Apple products are limited to essential functions and have a high recognition factor. Apple's products look different and are different from the mass, which a further competitive advantage of the company. These are only a few reasons for the success of the company, even more important is the company's innovative product range for several decades. The company has recognized weak signals and requirements of the industries and perceived opportunities.

3.2. The correlation between Apple's innovative product range and success

Apple products are not radically different, latest products have just small added innovative Additions and are characterized through a high design.

The balanced product portfolio of Apple Inc. includes innovative products and grants financial security.

The iPhone is just the latest example. Apple Inc. had previously caused attention with the Mac Computer, iPad and the iPod. For instance, Apple introduced the Macintosh Computer on the market, which had its own design and brand recognition, while other manufacturers sold large grey boxes as a computer. Such innovations helped the company to differentiate itself from the competitors.

In the mid- nineties the operating system was overhauled by competitors and other products scored on the market. Apple quickly re-oriented and introduced the practical and hand-held IPod, which attracted many buyers. Furthermore, the company offered a free iTunes software, which allowed the administration of music.

The next products, which had conquered the market with immensely speed were the iPhone and the iPad. Above all, the iPhone deserves special attention, because *"This innovation piece of technology has taken the world by storm. The convergence of cell phones and other technologies has been happening for some time. The Smart Phones have found the market of combining PDA functions along with all other cell phone functions. However, it is the iPhone that has taken these functions such as the camera, music, web browsing, text, GPS navigation, and yes of course voice communication and blended them all together so seamlessly into a great user experience. The Safari web browser providers the user with a full web browser page, rather than the limited mobile version of the Smart Phones"* (Maria Bernabo, 2009, Technological convergence throughout the eras: Part 2 – Cellular and computers, Business Strategy Series, Volume 10, Number 1, p12-18).

A simple classification of Apple's products can be shown in a Boston Consulting Group Matrix , like in Figure 2.

Especially, the iPhone as a "Star Product" and the iPad as a "Cash Cow" are the two main gears of the company, which grant a long-term business success. The iPhone has a tremendous unique selling point and it has become a social obligation to have an iPhone.

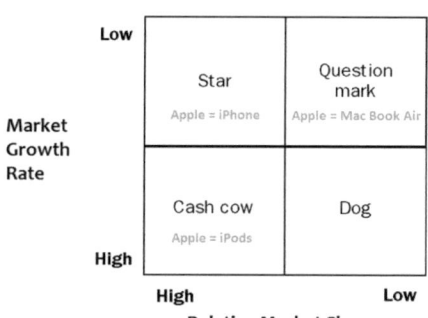

Figure 2, Boston Consulting Group Matrix

One of many success factors is the user friendliness of Apple's products. The devices are expensive, but have a striking design and clients can rely on high quality. No other company manages the production of simple or high value products as well as Apple. The power of innovation is derived by a radical simplification and *"Another reason why the iPhone is so revolutionary is due to the fact that it was created by Apple, a computer and software company. Every other phone on the market has been created by phone manufactures, such as Qualcomm, Motorola, and LG."* (Maria Bernabo, 2009, Technological convergence throughout the eras: Part 2 – Cellular and computers, Business Strategy Series, Volume 10, Number 1, p12-18)

4. Innovation and change

4.1. The differences between innovation and change

In some cases, innovations occur suddenly, but normally the process of emergence is planned, organized, managed and controlled by people or an organisation.

These groups create innovations intentionally, they are pursuing by the creation of new and improved outputs and the introduction of a "renewal" in a positive way. New technological innovations replace older innovations, this is illustrated by the S-curve in Figure 3, which represents the correlation between a new technology cycle, which is *" a cycle that begins with the 'birth' of a new technology and ends when that technology reaches its limits and is replaced by a newer, substantially better technology."* (Williams and McWilliams, 2010, MGMT, p130-147).

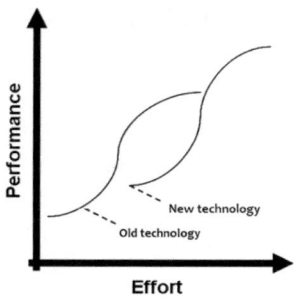

Figure 3, S- curve

The new technology could be for example the iPod, which has replaced the disc man. In this context, it should be considered, that length of technology cycles can vary. For example, the technological cycle of the iPhone is getting shorter and shorter.

Thus, the process of innovation can be understood as an ongoing process, which usually produces positive outputs. These outputs are mostly in businesses: satisfaction of consumer needs, the improvement of a product or service, the increase in shareholder value and sales increases.

Innovations require an investment in research and development and are associated with an industry- dependent uncertainty. However, a large financial reflux can occur through the investment. On the other hand, a change does not need an additional investment.

Sustainable innovations are rarely without a massive change in the business processes. This process should be understood as a matter of the whole organisation, thus the need for change is intended.

Companies can prepare prospective "Innovative leaps", therefore is a change in the management chain within a company necessary.

It is conceivable that there is no change without innovation and no innovation without a change and *"at the same time, many changes within an organization occur without intentionally of direct benefit but are merely adjustments which result from routine changes in internal or external environment conditions."*(Colin Hargie and Dennis Tourish, 1996, MCB University Press, Corporate Communications: An International Journal, Volume 1, Number 2, p3-11).

As already indicated, a change mostly occurs unexpectedly in an internal and external environment. Almost, all companies are surrounded by an external and dynamic environment, which is minted by a high rate of change and other companies are surrounded by an external stable environment, which implies that the rate of change is slow. These external alterations cause external disturbances which affect a company. Quite the cybernetic sense, less competitive firms have to react to compensate external disturbances and other companies such as Apple Inc. have to react less. Innovative companies are more immune against changes. They have already involved innovation as a fundamental prerequisite in the corporate culture.

Companies, which are out of balance by disturbances, are trying to restore its old or a new equilibrium. Changes occur even as an external disturbance, as well as an internal disturbance by the internal environment, which is defined as "the events and trends inside an organisation that affect management, employees and organisational cultures." (Williams and McWilliams, 2010, MGMT, p130-147). Ultimately, both types of change are negative, because both types of change are not intentionally and require adjustments, which are sophisticated.

4.2.   The similarities between innovation and change

Innovation and change represent an alteration, which is most positive associated by innovation and negatively by change. In both cases, an adaptation of the company is required. It may happens, that the business operational and organization changes because of expansion or by the introduction of an innovative product. Both situations represent a change and challenge for the company. If the company expanded and new departments are necessary, this kind of change must be accepted by the workforce and can be tackled through the use of effective change management.

The prospective problems of organizational innovation can be limited by effective communication, because *"A well developed, clearly formulated communication strategy is a vital prerequisite which should form a central part in any plan to carry through organizational innovation."* (Colin Hargie and Dennis Tourish, 1996, MCB University Press, Corporate Communications: An International Journal, Volume 1, Number 2, p3-11).

5. Conclusion

In summary, innovation can be described as the improvement of the existing performance, in which the correct usage of innovations guarantees long term growth and earnings increases for a company, even an Economic Value Added in value- oriented companies. Especially, through the invention and successful market introduction of "star products" with a unique selling point, an increased demand can be observed and companies are quickly able to take the advantage of economies of scale. Such companies are better immunized against the market dynamic and gain a range of competitive advantages, which facilitates the acquisition of new shareholders.

6. List of reference

Williams, C and McWilliams, A, 2010, MGMT, 1st Asia-Pacific edn, Cengage Learning Australia, South Melbourne

Chris Freeman, 1982, The Economics of Industrial Innovation, 2nd edition, Printer, London

Axel John, 1999, Successful market innovation, European Journal of Innovation Management, Volume 2 , Number 1, p6-11

Maria Bernabo, 2009, Technological convergence throughout the eras: Part 2 – Cellular and computers, Business Strategy Series, Volume 10, Number 1, p12-18

Colin Hargie and Dennis Tourish, 1996, MCB University Press, Corporate Communications: An International Journal, Volume 1, Number 2, p3-11

http://www.squidoo.com/bcggrowthsharematrix

http://www.apple.com/

http://innovationzen.com/blog/2006/08/17/innovation-management-theory-part-4/